'I'M THE GREATEST!'

THE WIT AND HUMOUR OF MUHAMMAD ALI

'I'M TH
GREATE

...ST!

THE WIT AND HUMOUR OF MUHAMMAD ALI

Cartoons: ROY ULLYETT and JON
Photo Captions: ROY HEELAS
Text Compilation: DILLIBE ONYEAMA
& JOHN WALTERS

LESLIE FREWIN of LONDON

First published 1975 by
Leslie Frewin Publishers Limited,
Five Goodwin's Court,
Saint Martin's Lane,
London WC2N 4LL, England.

This book is printed in Latinesque,
photoset, printed and bound in Great Britain by
Weatherby Woolnough, Sanders Road, Wellingborough,
Northamptonshire.

ISBN 0 85632 142 7

'Essentially, every black boxing champion until Muhammad Ali had been a puppet, manipulated by whites in his private life to control his public image . . . With the coming of Muhammad Ali, the puppet-master was left with a handful of strings to which his dancing doll was no longer attached.'

—*ELDRIDGE CLEAVER: Soul on Ice*

'Ali can retire from the ring but he may never be able to retire as "the people's champ".'

—*The Negro Digest*

'Ali! . . . Ali! . . . Ali! . . .'

—*BERNADETTE DEVLIN*—at the ringside of one of Ali's fights.

'Man, I was perfect!'

—*MUHAMMAD ALI* (After beating George Foreman in 1974 and regaining the heavyweight crown)

'The Black Explosion'
—*London Daily Express*

ILLUSTRATIONS

CONTENTS

CASSIUS CLAY?
Mohammed Ali?
BLACK MUSLIM?
Draft Dodger?
BIG MOUTH ?
SPARTAN
BUT NEVER DOUBT HE IS The CHAMP.

INTRODUCTION

With a personality that is as changeable as the British weather, Muhammad Ali, or, if you prefer it, Cassius Clay, has become not just the most unusual boxer in history, but one of the most unusual of human beings.

Born in Louisville, Kentucky, on 17th January 1942, and married with four children, he was once hated by the world because of his own efflorescent image of himself – The Greatest. The Prettiest. The Fastest. But since he has more than lived up to that image, the world has had no choice but to come to love his blatant and often outrageous conceit. This, irrespective of his amazingly contradictory character. He has attacked materialism and ostentation, yet he fills his garage with a Rolls-Royce, a Cadillac, an antique car, a camper and a Lincoln – and the world loves him for it! He has slated former heavyweight champion Floyd Patterson for living in a white neighbourhood instead of a black one, yet he buys a mansion in an exclusive white suburb – and the world loves him for it! He has defined boxing as a degrading sport chiefly indulged in for the white man's entertainment, yet was ready to sign for a whimsey fight against the seven-foot basketball player Wilt Chamberlain – and the world loves him for it! He is a sincere member of the Black Muslim religious movement which generally regards all white people as devils, yet it is well known that he has a number of close white friends – and the world loves him for it! He has said that he is not obsessed with fighting and that he uses it 'as a platform in order to get to my people', yet he screamed for vengeance and a return fight when he was beaten by Joe Frazier and Ken Norton – and the world, needless to say, loved him, too, for this contradiction of character.

Known the world over by people who have never heard of such celebrities as the Queen of England, Hitler, Kennedy or Nixon, Muhammad Ali is unquestionably the most outstanding sporting personality of our age. Not only because he has been the only heavyweight to use the ring like a ballet-dancer, combining speed with grace; not only because of the amusing verse he spouts to predict the round in which he will destroy his opponent; not only because of his brilliant showmanship; not only because he is 6ft 3ins and fifteen stones of black beauty; not only because he repudiated the identity white America gave him – Cassius Clay – and took on a new identity – Muhammad Ali; not only because he battled against the Supreme Court rather than oppose the principles of his religion and fight in Vietnam, and *won* – but also because of his incredible sense of bubbling fun and humour. If there is one thing the world loves most about Muhammad Ali, it is that sense of humour, particularly his quick-wittedness, and his boyish gift of derision. One never quite knows if he is laughing at *himself* or whether he is deadly serious. In public, the crowds always assemble, threatening to crush him to death with their admiration, firing questions designed to provoke replies that will send them into fits of laughter. They are *never* disappointed. Ali's trainer, Angelo Dundee, has said of him: *He's learned a lot, travelling around the world, being with people – little people – big people – that's his college. He doesn't learn from books. The truth is he never really learned to read, but he sucks in knowledge, information, ideas like an elephant sucks in water. And he trumpets it all out just like an elephant, too.*

He also trumpets out wit and humour like a music hall comic, and many go along with his description of himself as The Greatest –

certainly in terms of wit! And none can doubt his immaculate prowess as 'The Champ of Champs'.

This book, then, is a compilation of Muhammad Ali's humour combined with the wit of celebrated cartoonists, Roy Ullyett and Jon, with journalist Roy Heelas. At the time of writing, Ali threatens to star in his first film. It should be funnier than a Woody Herman comedy – and assuredly will be if Muhammad Ali has his way. As, equally assuredly, he will . . .

He fits no pattern. He is the total nonconformist. And love him or hate him – you have to concede he is one of the great *individuals* of our age.

1. ON HIMSELF

With typical modesty, Muhammad Ali first introduced himself to the world as The Greatest in 1960, after winning the Gold Medal in the Light-heavyweight Boxing in the Rome Olympics. A team-mate recalls: 'If there had been an election for mayor of our Olympic village in Rome, Cassius would have won in a landslide victory. He was all over the place, talking with everybody, teasing, joking, breaking down barriers – a born ambassador.' Returning to his hometown, Louisville, the 'ambassador' strutted the streets, admiring his reflection in the store-front windows before turning to the adoring crowd to announce:

Look at me, am I not beauty? Inhale me, am I not perfume?

* * *

To a fan in a crowd who yelled, 'Gee, you're so cool, Cassius!':

'I'm the Greatest!'

You know, man, you lucky, you seen me here in living colour.

* * *

When in March 1963 publicity for his fight with top contender Doug Jones was reduced to radio and television because of a 95-day-old New York newspaper strike:

This is unfair to the many boxing fans New York city has. Now they won't be able to read about the great Cassius Clay.

★ ★ ★

As his excuse for disastrously failing the Mental Arithmetic questions fired at him at the Army Induction Centre in Florida in 1964:

I said I was the greatest, not the smartest.

★ ★ ★

To a large crowd of fans in a New York street:

I whip my opponents so bad that even my pretty kid daughter watched me on television and said: 'Gee, look at ma Daddy whup that man. That man must have done something real bad for ma Daddy to whup him so bad.'

★ ★ ★

When in May 1963 he came to London to fight the then British Heavyweight Champion Henry Cooper, he was interviewed by commentator David Coleman on television and walked out of the show when Coleman told him: 'I must admit, I'm a Cooper fan – and so are most of the British people. And I think you talk too much.' Ali's retort:

I don't have to be on your programme. You aren't doing me any favour. I should be in bed resting. I'm going.

* * *

In late 1963 he made an album – I AM THE GREATEST – a long pastiche of poems and skits composed wholly in terms of his impending fight with the then World Champion Sonny Liston. It went thus:

This is the legend of Cassius Clay,
The most beautiful fighter in the world today.
He talks a great deal and brags indeed
Of a muscular punch that's incredible in speed.
This brash young boxer is something to see
And the heavyweight championship is his destiny.
He is *the greatest!*
This kid fights great, he's got speed and endurance;
But if you sign to fight him, increase your insurance.
This kid's got a left, this kid's got a right;

'I'm the Greatest!'

If he hits you once you'll sleep for the night.
And as you lie on the floor while the Ref counts ten
You pray that you won't have to fight me again.
The fistic world was a-stalling wary;
With a champ like me, then things had to be real.
Then someone with colour, someone with dash,
Brought fight fans a-running with cash –
CASSIUS CLAY!

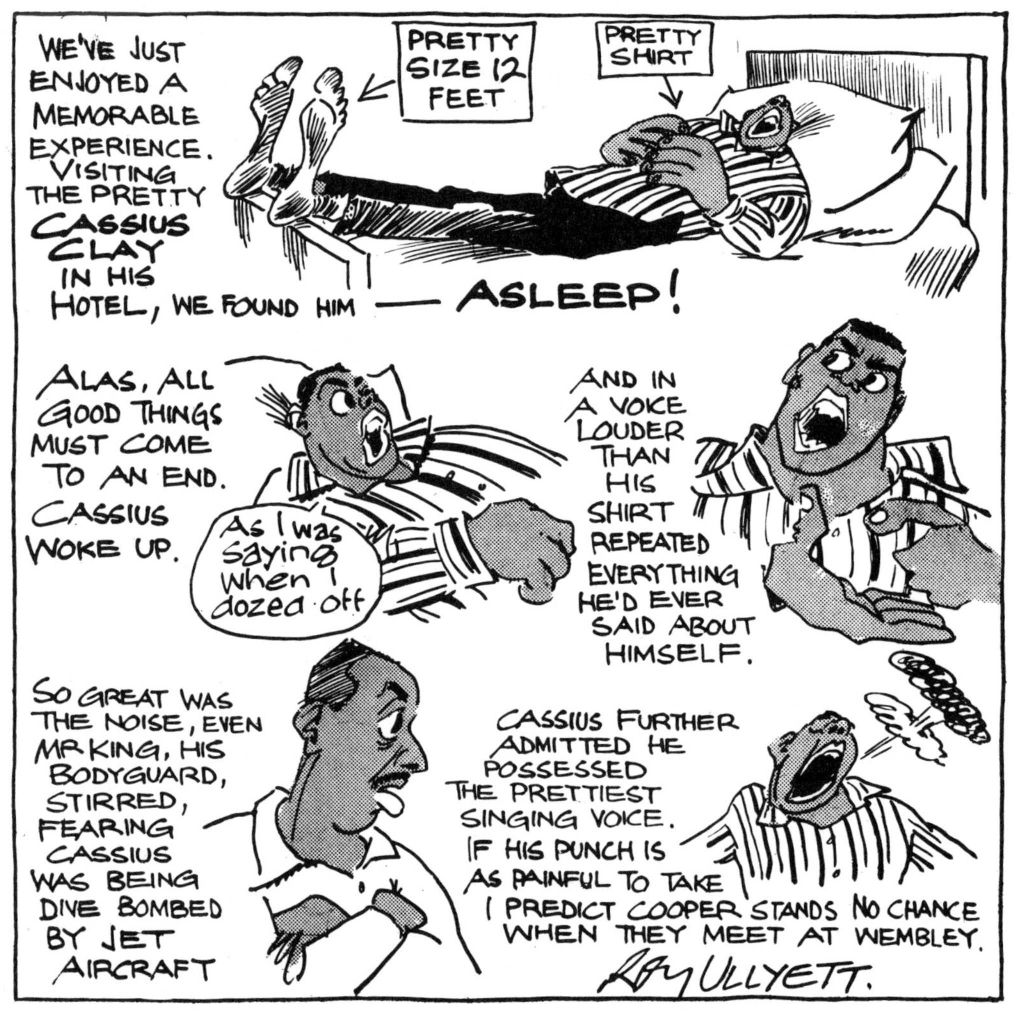

During one of his autograph sessions a week before his fight with Sonny Liston, he was only prepared to sign autographs for one dollar each, the money to go to three black kid musicians for bringing variety to the session. To one fan who was only prepared to put fifty cents into the musicians' large collection box:

Come on, man, don't put no fifty cents in there, get that dollar bill out. Think at all you're getting free here – the music's so fine and here you got Cassius Clay right here in front of you in living colour, the next heavyweight champion of the world, the man who's gonna put old man Liston in orbit.

★ ★ ★

At another autograph session, a muscularly-built fan, an ex-wrestler, came forward and shook his hand, and apparently squeezed too hard. Ali, pulling his hand away suddenly and wringing it, warned:

Don't ever squeeze a boxer's hand, man. That hand's worth about three hundred thousand dollars. You don't have to shake hands. You doing good just to lay eyes on me.

★ ★ ★

When surrounded by the Press after defeating Sonny Liston:

'I'm the Greatest!'

Look, I tried to tell you how great I was and you chumps wouldn't listen.

★ ★ ★

Asked what initially made him start to shoot off his mouth:

I began after watching Gorgeous George, the wrestler. I hear this white fellow say: 'I am the World's Greatest Wrestler. I cannot be defeated. I am the Greatest! I am King! If that sucker mess up my pretty waves in my hair, I'm gonna kill him. I am King. If that sucker whups me, I gonna get the next jet to Russia. I cannot *be defeated!' When he was in the ring, everybody* boooooooed *and* boooooooed. *Oh, everybody just* boooooooed. *And I was mad. And I looked around and I saw everybody was mad. I saw 15,000 people coming to see this man get beat. And his talking did it. And I said, this is a* goooooooood *idea!*

★ ★ ★

Asked what he feels like when he is in the ring:

Whenever I step into the ring only one thing matters . . . that I end up the boss. Just ask my sparring partners Jimmy Ellis and Cody Jones. They got the bruises to prove it!

★ ★ ★

After his spectacular thrashing of the giant Negro Ernie Terrel in March 1967, Ali was confronted by an American TV commentator.

'Muhammad Ali,' said the commentator, 'you were simply great. Joe Louis told me to tell you so; he's sorry he couldn't stop to tell you himself.' Ali shouted indignantly, with a wave of the hand:

I don't need neither Joe nor no one to tell me I'm great. I've been telling you that for the past six years, haven't I?

★ ★ ★

Asked if he would encourage his sons to take up boxing as a profession:

No. The odds of making a good living out of it are about 100,000 to one. I'll tell them to get their brains together and get educated. Ain't no point them boxing unless they gonna be great like me.

★ ★ ★

When in April 1967 he was stripped of his title for refusing induction into the Armed Forces and was told that the World Boxing Association had created an elimination to pick its next champion:

Let them heve the elimination bouts. Let the man who wins go to the backwoods of Georgia and Alabama or to Sweden or Africa. Let him stick his head in an elementary school, let him walk down a back alley at night. Let him stop under a street lamp where some small boys are playing and let him say: 'What's my name?' and see what they say. Everybody knows me and knows I am the champion. You see, they know who the real champion is and all the rest is my sparring partners.

* * *

Before his fight with the formidable 'White Hope' Jerry Quarry in October 1970, he was asked by a fan in a large crowd: 'Are you afraid?' Ali's reply:

I'm nervous, not afraid. But it's not the man in the opposite corner that makes me nervous – it's all those people waitin' in Holland and Philadelphia, all those people watching the fight all the way in Moscow. If the satellite don't work or somethin' an' the people are disappointed, that *makes me nervous.*

★ ★ ★

At the same autograph session, he spots a towering basketball star in the crowd and gives him an introduction:

There he is, folks, the great Elgin Bayler! Someone corrects him – it's Walt Bellamy. Ali smiles and replies: *Sorry folks, all those spook basketball players look alike.* Bellamy comes up and shakes hands with Ali, who indicates how the former's height towers above his own 6ft 3ins. *Now if* he *could fight, that would scare me!*

★ ★ ★

In December 1970, though he knocked out Argentine Oscar Bonavena in the fifteenth round, he failed to do so in the round he had predicted – the ninth. In fact, he was almost knocked out himself in that round. Later, in the dressing room, with a bruise around one eye and blood seeping from a small wound on his lips, he sighed:

'I'm the Greatest!'

Guess I ain't so pretty no more. Funny, when I was predictin' the ninth round, I never thought I came close to predictin' on myself.

★ ★ ★

His poem for his 29th birthday:

I've been away for three and a half years taking a rest
Now I'm back in the ring and I'm the best.

★ ★ ★

When offered half a million dollars to act as the world's first black heavyweight boxing champion Jack Johnson (an admirer of white women) in the film *The Great White Hope,* Ali refused. His reason:

I ain't appearing on no screen with no white woman.

★ ★ ★

Asked if he would turn his Supreme Court victory into a motion picture:

Don't have to. I'm livin' my movie every day.

★ ★ ★

Asked by TV interviewer Michael Parkinson in an interview: 'Do you ever get people trying to pick fights with you to try and prove themselves?' Ali, with amused surprise:

If anyone even dreams *he can beat me, he had better wake up and apologise.*

★ ★ ★

'I'm the Greatest!'

His farewell message to Michael Parkinson at the end of the programme:

I like your show and I like your style
But your pay's so bad I won't be back for a while.

When in March 1973 he was invited to visit China:

The Red Chinese Government has invited me. I will go to the same places as Nixon went and see the same people – only I may get to see some people he didn't. I'm known everywhere.

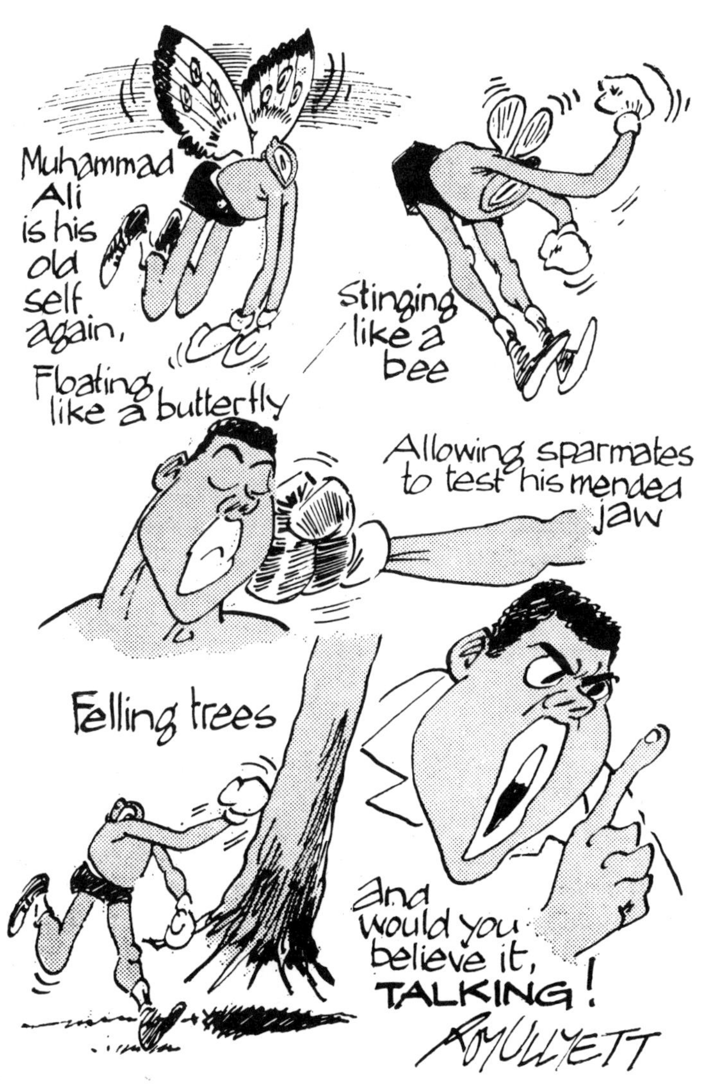

'I'm the Greatest!'

His latest claim is that he is the greatest in the kitchen. Some of the rules of his kitchen are:

PLEASE KEEP OUT – except on the express permission of the cook.

No remarks at all will be tolerated concerning the blackening of toast, the weakening of soup or the strength of the garlic stew.

What goes in stews and soups is NOBODY'S damn business.

If you must stick your finger in something, please do it in the garbage disposal.

ANYONE bringing guests in for dinner without prior notice will be awarded thwacks on the skull with a sharp object.

★ ★ ★

2. ON SONNY LISTON

The world will always remember Ali's first world-title fight with Sonny Liston in February 1964 as one of boxing's greatest upsets, since the fearsome stony-faced Liston (nicknamed by Ali 'The Ugly Bear') was thought invincible by many and was expected to spank the obstreperous Ali like a strict father would spank a wayward son. But Ali confounded the army of sceptics by using Liston as a human punch-bag and making him look slow, tired and old. It was an incredible fight that ended after Liston failed to come out for the seventh round. But Ali really won two fights – the battle of fists and that of wit. The world will never forget the taunting Ali showered over Liston before their fight – Liston's usual reply being a cold silence and a sullen stare. Asked how he would deal with Liston in the fight, Ali replied:

I'll demolish Liston in eight rounds, and he'll be in a worser fix if I predict six. I'll give him talking lessons and boxing lessons. What he needs most is falling down lessons. That big black bear ain't gonna beat me, 'cause I'm gonna float like a butterfly, sting like a bee.

* * *

He invaded Liston's training camp, announcing:

This is the bear-hunting season! (to Liston) *You big ugly bear! You're the chump and I'm the champ!*

* * *

Asked by a fan at an autograph session if he really believed he would beat Liston:

They down there right now getting Medicare ready for that old man, and if I hit him in the mouth he's gonna need Denticare.

* * *

Re-enacting an imaginary encounter with Liston to a group of newsmen in his hotel suite:

I'm gonna say to him: 'You big ugly bear, I ain't gonna fight you on no September thirtieth; I'm gonna fight you right now. Right here. You too ugly to run loose, you big ugly bear. You so ugly that when you cry, the tears run down the back of your head. You so ugly you have to sneak up on the mirror so it won't run off the wall.' Then Liston says (mimicking Liston's low, gruffy voice): 'Come over here and sit on my knee, little boy, and I'll give you your orange juice,' and I pull back my right fist and three guys

hold me back and keep me from throwing it at Liston, and I'm hollering 'Lemme go!', and I'm telling them out of the side of my mouth, 'You better not *lemme go.'*

'I'm the Greatest!'

A week before his fight with Liston, a young white soldier approached him as he was signing autographs and asked him: 'Where are you gonna go after Sonny Liston whips you? I got some travel folders right here.'

'*Boy,*' answered Sli, '*you talk about travelling. I want you to go to that fight, 'cause you gonna see the launching of a human satellite – Sonny Liston.*'

'I got some travel folders,' said the soldier. 'You better look 'em over. I can get you a mask, too.'

'*You gonna bet against me?*' asked Ali in surprise.

'Every cent I can get my hands on,' replied the soldier.
'Man,' said Ali, laughing, *'you better save your money, 'cause there's gonna be a total eclipse of the Sonny.'*

* * *

After his defeat of Liston, he told newsmen:

I feel sorry for Liston. You people put too much load on him. You built him up too big and now he has such a long way to fall.

* * *

Commenting on the time he was watching a replay of his fight with Liston on BBC television:

At first I had to ask who the fast heavyweight was and then I discovered it was myself. So I sat and saw myself pounding into Liston, and every time I hit him in the film I gave a bonus punch with my right fist into my left palm. I enjoyed every minute, watching the class and the range, and all those pretty jabs. Then came that moment when Liston went back into his corner and his trainer was saying: 'Get out there, man!' And Liston was saying: 'No, I'm staying right here on my stool!'

Yea, man! I float like a butterfly, I sting like a bee,
Muhammad is Champion – Muhammad is me.

* * *

At the Ringside
Lewiston
OTHER THAN LISTON STANDING UPRIGHT FOR THE NATIONAL ANTHEM, HE DIDN'T SHOW MUCH FORM
IN ONE MINUTE, WE SAW HIM ON HIS BACK
ON HIS SIDE
ON HIS KNEES BUT NOT ONCE ON HIS HEAD
AND HE'D PRACTISED THAT ONE IN TRAINING
YOU SHOULD HAVE HEARD THE CROWD HOLLER THEIR ABUSE .... SO RUDE TOO
AFTER THAT, I'LL NEVER ACCUSE CLAY OF SHOUTING. BY COMPARISON HE COOS LIKE A DOVE
Roy ULLYETT.

3. ON JOE FRAZIER

Joe Frazier (nicknamed 'Smokin' Joe') was the first boxer to defeat Ali in March 1971, though Ali got his revenge in their return bout in January 1974. Many will always remember Frazier not only because he was the first man to temporarily close the 'Louisville Lip', but also because Ali used no other as a butt for his wit as much as Frazier. Before their first fight, the general feeling of the American press was that Frazier would win. To this, Ali's reply at a press conference was:

All you fellows with your typewriters, drinkin' every night, pickin' against me, never learned ya lesson with Liston, did ya? Frazier says he's gonna come out smokin'; smokin's bad for the lungs – gives you cancer. I'm gonna bring my fire extinguisher with me next Monday night, straighten this mess out once and for all.

* * *

Asked whether Frazier had a chance:

Frazier's got two chances: slim and none.

Commenting on Frazier's love for pop-music:

Since Joe Frazier has a band (a group called 'The Knockouts') *I got something for him – musically speaking:*

If Joe Frazier don't be sharp
He'll be flat.

★ ★ ★

Pretending angry scorn for Frazier at an autograph session:

He's got some nerve announcin' a victory party already. I heard he invited Duke Ellington an' his trio. Frazier can't even dance. Ain't got no rhythm. They say he got lots of endurance, but he better be taking out life insurance.

★ ★ ★

In his hotel suite a few days before the fight, he walked around the room barefoot, telling a select audience:

Let me tell you somethin', the mind is powerful. If people could only see how much more powerful the mind is than the body. People like Frazier could never see it. (imitates Frazier's deep nasal voice) *'Oh, I owe everything to boxin'! If it wasn't for boxin' I'd be back in the ghetto!' All that stuff.*

★ ★ ★

While watching Frazier singing on television with his pop group:

Can't even sing. Last thing a fighter should be is a singer. Who wants to see him as a romantic movie star? No big man can play love scenes with itty bitty girls and say (in low, rumbling voice) *'I loves you'. You need a small, neat, compact man to say* (in high falsetto) *'I love yooooooouuuuu'.*

★ ★ ★

Asked how he would deal with Frazier in their fight:

Joe Frazier's gonna come out smoking
And I ain't gonna be joking,
I'll be pecking and a-poking
Pouring water on his smoking.
This might shock and amaze ya,
But, I'm gonna re-tire Joe Frazier.

★ ★ ★

At the medical examination before the fight, the state physician was trying to keep Ali quiet long enough to get the examination under way.

'Now let's be serious,' pleaded the physician. 'Have you had any headaches?'

'HEADACHES?!' shouted Ali, looking round at the assembled newsmen in feigned amazement. *'I don't get headaches; I give my opponents headaches.'*

'Will you please touch the floor twenty times?' asked the physician.

'You want me to touch the floor twenty times! Let's see you do it first.'

When he finally did carry out the bending exercise, he was asked to extend his arms horizontally.
'When I stretch out my arms,' Ali replied, *'I'm used to holding them up this way!'* He raised his arms in the victory salute.
The physician took out his tongue depresser.
'Do I have *to open my mouth?'* protested Ali.
Later, when he was stretched out on the examination table, the doctor thumped him on the chest.
Ali: *'Did you hit Frazier that hard?'*

★ ★ ★

To a crowd on the day of his fight with Frazier:

You know, I'm scared. No kiddin', I'm really scared. I'm scared Joe Frazier won't show up tonight.

★ ★ ★

After his defeat by Frazier, he made a forecast:

Next time there'll be no doubt.
For next time he'll be out.

★ ★ ★

He has always maintained that he really won that first fight with Frazier, as have many of his fans. Frazier's puffed face and swollen eyes were evidence that he had suffered more in the

This clarifies the situation. Mr Frazier has convincingly established himself as the recognised World Heavyweight Champion I could WHUP WITH ONE HAND!
BIG FIGHT
FRAZIER K.O's ELLIS
ROY ULLYETT.

fight than Ali; it was believed, too, that the fight had taken a lot out of Frazier. His 2nd-round knockout by George Foreman in January 1973, his first defeat ever, proved this. Ali's reaction on hearing of Frazier's knockout:

Gee! I didn't realise I beat him so bad. I knew I beat Frazier but now the people can see how bad I beat him.

★ ★ ★

Crosstalk in August 1973 between Ali and Frazier, as told to a Press reporter:

FRAZIER: Ali is too busy making bread against bums to worry about a *real* fight.

ALI: *Joe* who, *did you say? . . . Oh, Frazier. Yeah, I remember him. He's the one that leads with his face all the time.*

FRAZIER: Ali *talks* a great fight, but you just try to pin him down to agreement terms for a re-match.

ALI: *I suggest the next time we meet should be at the Cape Kennedy launching pad. Frazier will be the first black astronaut when I get my uppercut to work.*

FRAZIER: I am always amused by Ali. I beat him fair and square in our title fight and yet to hear him describe the fight now you would think I had not landed a single blow.

ALI: I've got a crowded schedule. Chuvalo in Vancouver on May 1, Al Lewis in Dublin on June 12, Jerry Quarry in Las Vegas June 26. I can accommodate Frazier any time after that.

FRAZIER: I'll fight Ali when it suits me and my accountant. Not before.

ALI: Name the time and the place and I'll be there. Tell all my wonderful friends to stand in the street and look to the sky and they'll see Joe Frazier rising ever so high.

★ ★ ★

His reply when told by a Press reporter before his second fight with Frazier: 'Joe Frazier is fitter for you than when he fought Foreman or Bugner.':

Good. He's gonna need to be. He is up against the master. I'm so fast I'll hit him before God get's the news. He'll see so many gloves he'll think he's fighting an octopus.

★ ★ ★

In a television confrontation with Joe Frazier a week before their second fight:

FRAZIER: I'm sure gonna come out smokin', man, you better believe it.

ALI: *Sure I believe it. And I'll be pouring water on your smokin'.*

FRAZIER: I'm gonna finish you right off this time. Ain't no point you trying to impress everybody with your punching power on the bag. The bag can't hit back, man. It can't hit back.

ALI: *You sound like you're trying to make a point. Everybody knows the bag can't hit back.*

* * *

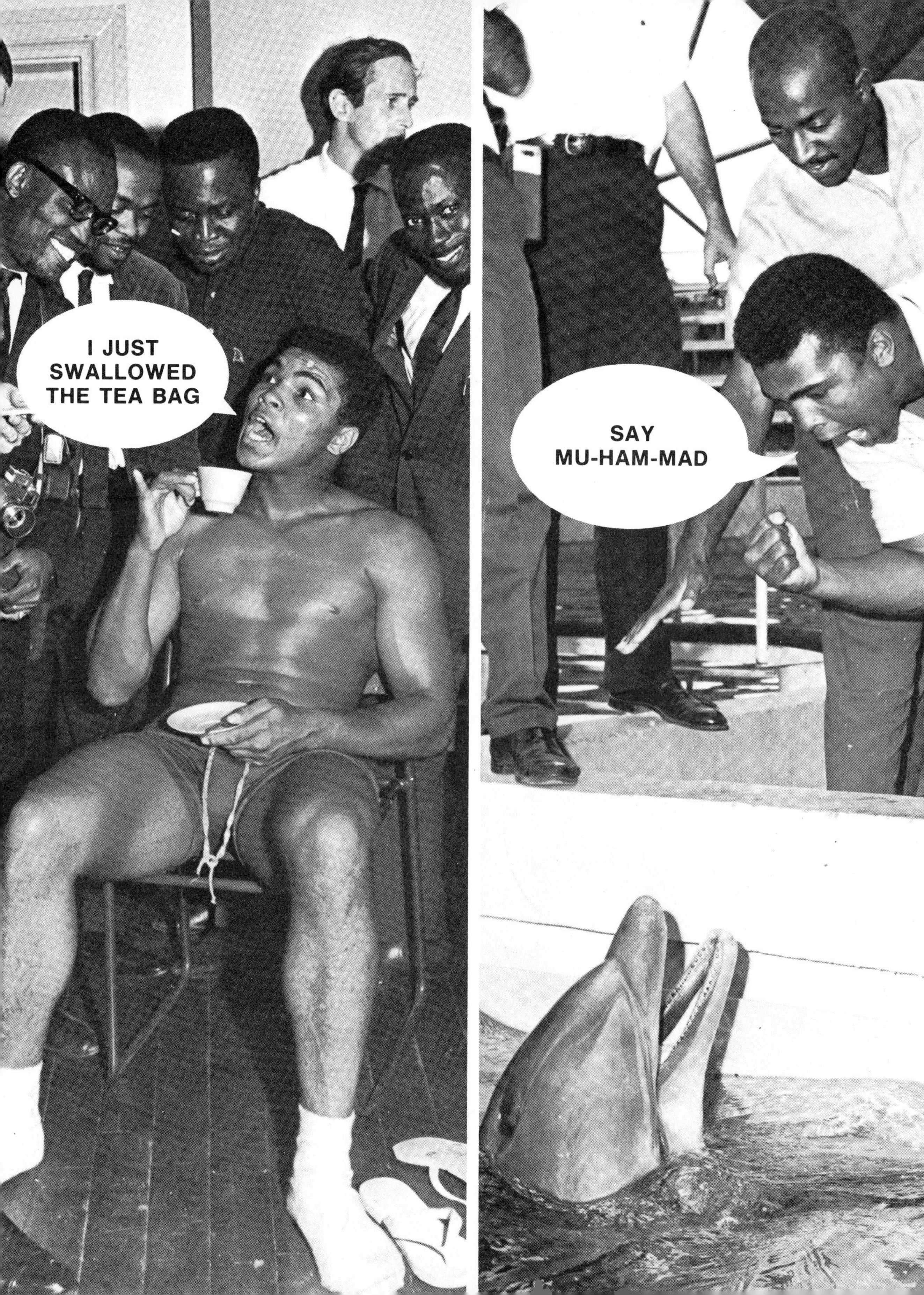
I JUST
SWALLOWED
THE TEA BAG
SAY
MU-HAM-MAD

FRIENDS . . .
QUICK, LET ME OUTTA HERE — I LEFT THE BATH WATER RUNNING!

SHOW US THAT TRICK WHERE YOU PUT THE CIGAR SIDEWAYS IN YOUR MOUTH . . .

I KNOW I DROPPED MY MODESTY SOMEWHERE AROUND HERE . . .

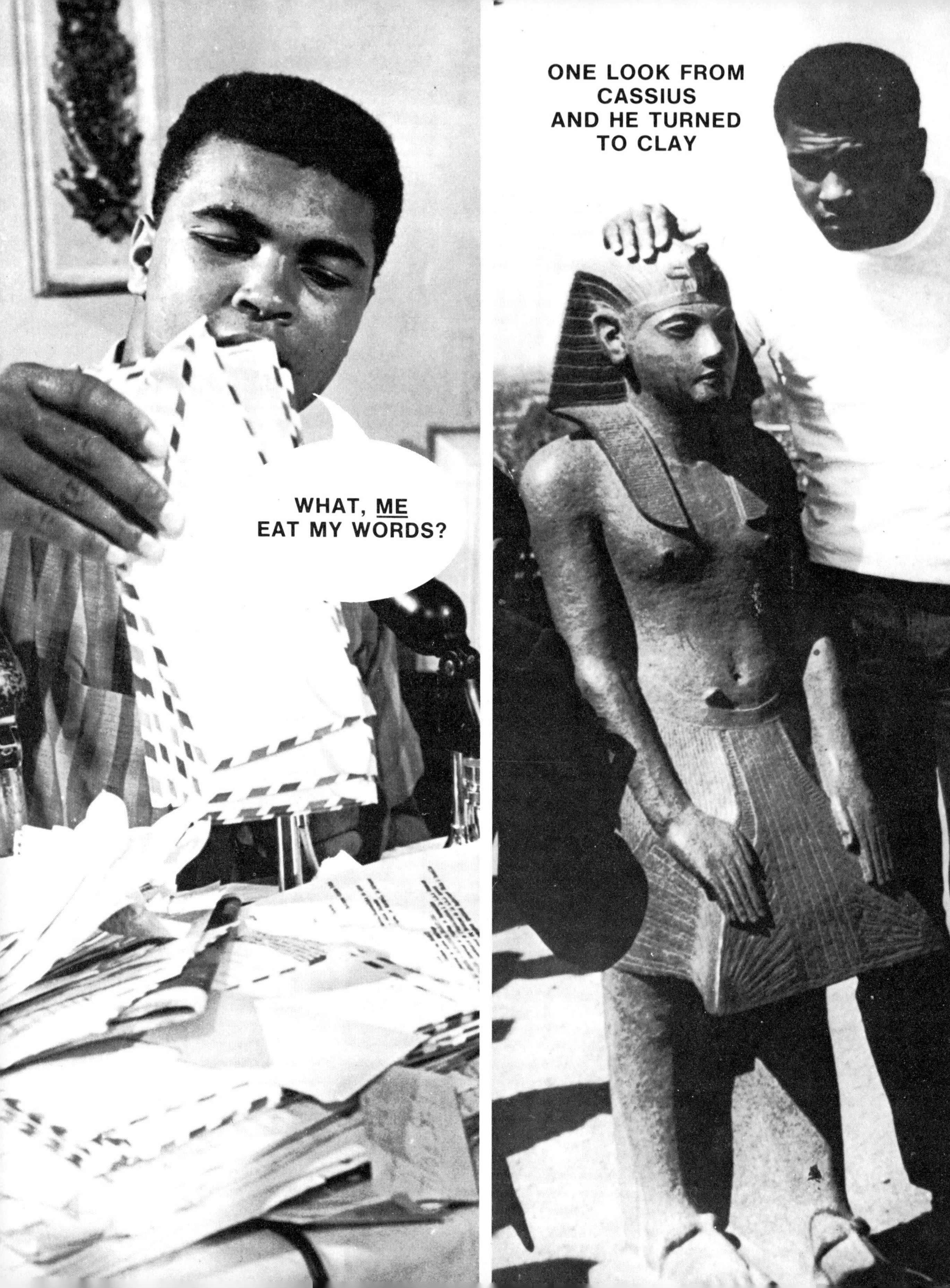
WHAT, ME
EAT MY WORDS?
ONE LOOK FROM
CASSIUS
AND HE TURNED
TO CLAY

DON'T CARE IF
THE EASTER PARADE IS
IMPORTANT, I STILL FEEL
SILLY IN THE SAME HAT
TWO YEARS RUNNING
SPARTAN

OK, I GOT IT NOW: YOU PUT YOUR RIGHT ARM IN, YOUR RIGHT ARM OUT . . .

THINKS:

GOVERNMENT WARNING:
THIS CAN HARM YOUR HEALTH
NO
SPARTAN

AIN'T NO FLY GONNA TALK BACK TO ME!
HI! THIS IS ALI IN ECHO VALLEY . . . ALI . . . ALI . . .

HIS BODY HAS TO BE WOUND UP — BUT HIS MOUTH WORKS BY PERPETUAL MOTION!
HEY! YOU'RE FINGER-LICKIN' GOOD!

4. ON BLACK OPPONENTS

[illegible] has always hated aeroplanes. So when in March 1961, he was asked whether he was nervous about his impending fight with 6ft 6ins, 226lbs black opponent Kolo Sabedong, the first black opponent taller and bigger than he was, his reply:

I'm not afraid to fight. I'm afraid of the flight.

★ ★ ★

October 1962 saw his fight with the very beefy and formidable black fighter Archie Moore, who said 'I'm gonna develop the "Lip-buttoner punch", specially designed for that fresh boy.' Ali, in rebuttal, came up with a poem:

Archie Moore has been living off the fat of the land.
I'm here to give him his pension plan.
When you come to the fight don't block aisle or door,
'Cause ya all going home after round four.

★ ★ ★

His prediction of his fight with Doug Jones in March 1963:

Jones likes to mix
So I'll let it go six.
If he talks jive,
I'll cut it to five.
And if he talks some more
I'll cut it to four.

★ ★ ★

After making his prediction he told a reporter:

It's all this running around that gets me. Last week or so it's been: 'Cassius will you be on my TV show?'; 'Cassius, will you cut a tape for radio?'; 'Cassius, will you pose for pictures?' Man, I'm tired. And all the time I gotta talk, you know. People expect it. Reporters say: 'We don't want to ask you questions, man. Just talk.' My mouth is tired.

★ ★ ★

After his fight with Doug Jones went the whole ten rounds, someone said: 'Clay almost didn't have the yen to finish the entire ten.' Ali's reply:

Well, I told you first that 'Jones likes to mix, and I'll let it go six', and then I said 'cut it to four', so four and six make ten, see?

★ ★ ★

When in 1964 former world heavyweight champion Floyd Patterson criticised Ali's beliefs in the Black Muslims:

I'll fight Patterson in a winner-take-all bout. I would give my purse to the Black Muslims, and Patterson could give his to the Catholic Church if he is the victor. I'll play with him for ten rounds. I will pow him. Then after I beat him, I'll convert him.

* * *

He nicknamed Patterson 'the Rabbit', and walked into Patterson's training quarters with a bag of carrots for 'the Rabbit' and started taunting him. A reporter asked Patterson: 'Do you get mad with these things?'

PATTERSON (quietly): Well, I'm happy that the heavyweight champ, Mister Clay, took time to——

ALI (shouting): That ain't my name. C'mon rabbit, what's my name?

PATTERSON (calmly): I was saying that I was happy to see Ali . . .

ALI (demandingly): The full name!

PATTERSON (losing patience): Well, Cassius Clay is the name he was born with!

ALI (mockingly): Don't be mad at me. I'm not the white man who chased you out from that white neighbourhood!

★ ★ ★

Before his fight against the ferocious black fighter Cleveland Williams – nicknamed 'The Big Cat':

I beat the Bear (Sonny Liston), *I beat the Hare* (Floyd Patterson) *and I'm gonna beat the Pussycat.*

★ ★ ★

Asked to predict a round for his April 1972 fight with the powerful Mac Foster:

It will be according to how he acts in the next few days. If he is a good man and does not talk too much, I might let it go several rounds.

★ ★ ★

About his opponent Bob Foster, light-heavyweight champion of the world, whom he fought in September 1972:

'A good clean fight, no pushing, no tripping . . .' Jon

He will fall in eight
Just to prove I'm great.

★ ★ ★

Asked if the high altitude of Nevada, where his fight with Bob Foster was to take place, would jeopardise his ability to keep up his dancing:

Altitude sickness is an old wives' tale. I'm fit enough to win a fight at the top of Mount Everest. Foster is the one who will be worried about height, because when I'm up on my toes, I'll look seven feet tall to him.

★ ★ ★

Asked by a reporter how good he reckoned George Foreman (the new heavyweight champion) was:

A pretty good amateur.

★ ★ ★

In March 1973, while training in a San Diego hotel for his fight with ex-marine Ken Norton, champion George Foreman entered and told him:
'I'll fight you when I'm ready.'
'That's all right, chump – I mean champ,' replied Ali; *'I don't need you. I'm making more money than you are. I don't need the title.'*
'If you can whip Joe Frazier's sparring partner, Ken Norton,' said Foreman, 'maybe you'll be ready for Frazier. Norton's better looking

'After Patterson there's a coloured heavy in Uganda who calls himself the greatest.'

than you.'
Feigning rage, Ali turned to the 600 crowd and announced: '*You're looking at the prettiest fighter in the world and the ugliest.*'
'Who's the ugliest?' asked Foreman.
'*Uh . . . I am,*' replied Ali – and turning to the crowd, said: '*I'll say anything he wants to get his name on a contract.*'

★ ★ ★

He was beaten for the second time in his life by the comparatively unknown Ken Norton. Asked to predict on their return fight in September 1973, Ali said:

You had better tell that Ken Norton that after I have finished with him this time, he's gonna be Ken Nothin'.

★ ★ ★

While training for his return fight with Norton, cutting down trees was part of his training:

Every time I chop down a tree, I yell 'Ken Norton!'

★ ★ ★

Asked to comment on Norton's announcement that he proposed to use positive thinking to help him beat Ali:

I don't blame him. 'Cause he's gonna need all the help he can get.

'If only Foster had cut his lip not his eye.'

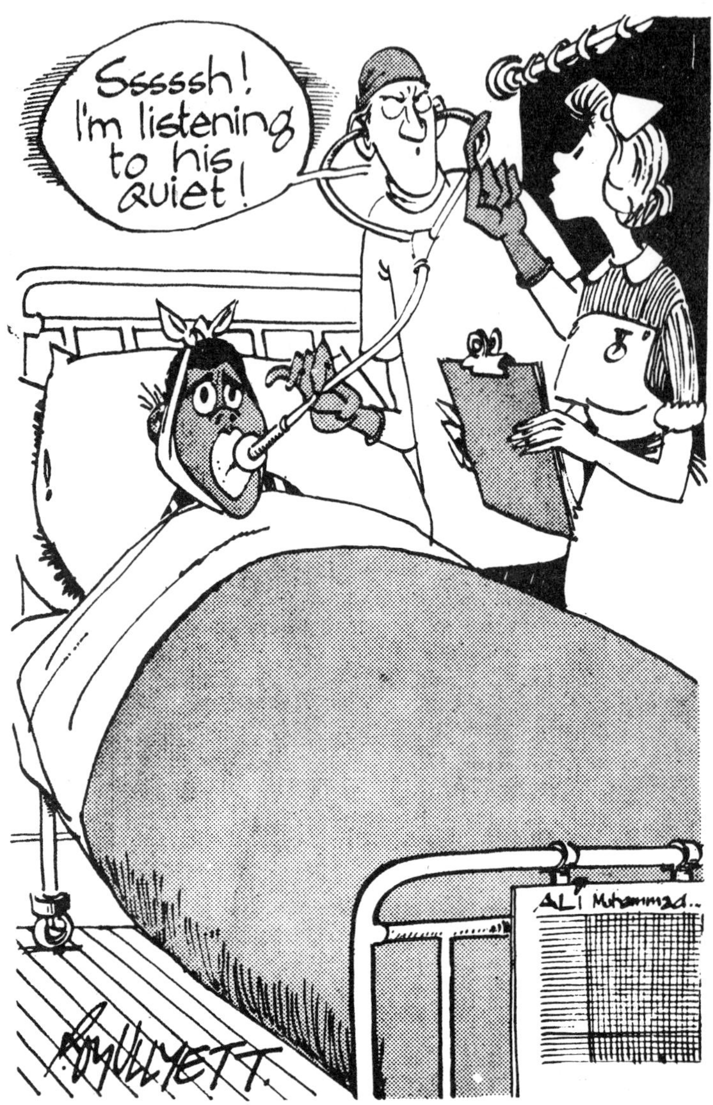

Asked what he thought of the fact that the odds were five to two on him despite the fact that Norton beat him last time and broke his jaw:

The guys who made the odds are smart. They figured that when I was in no shape to fight, Norton only just beat me. They realise that I can't be knocked out, that pain can't stop me. Norton keeps saying that he will start catching up with me after five or six rounds. That is defeatest talk, because if I did get tired dancing, and I can't see it happening, he will be even more tired from chasing.

5. ON WHITE OPPONENTS

Of Willie Besmanoff, a comparatively unknown German Jew and one of his first white professional opponents, Ali said:

I'm embarrassed to get in the ring with this unrated duck. I'm ready for top contenders.

★ ★ ★

When he came to London to fight Henry Cooper in 1963 and was told that the referee would be the sole judge:

It's the greatest system in the world. But I'm gonna make the referee's job easy by kayoing Cooper. Henry Cooper will think he's Gordon Cooper (the American astronaut) *when I put him in orbit.*

★ ★ ★

Of Henry Cooper:

He's a tramp, a bum and a cripple, not worth training for. I'll take him in five.

Previously he had said 'Henry will go in two. Or maybe one.' When a reporter asked him about the discrepancy, he replied:

I want to give the fans their money's worth.

"'ENERY WANTS YOU"
"UNCLE SAM WANTS YOU"
Roy Ullyett

Asked what he would do if Cooper did beat him:

If Cooper whups me, I'll get down on my hands and knees, crawl across the ring and kiss his feet. And then I'll take the next jet out to whichever country it happens to be going to, and I will be wearing a false moustache and beard.

* * *

He nicknamed George Chuvalo, the Canadian heavyweight champion, 'The Washerwoman', telling reporters: *'Did you ever see him swing? He throws his arms around just like a washerwoman.'*
One afternoon in February 1965, while Chuvalo was training for his fight with Floyd Patterson, Ali walked into his training camp with a mop and pail and presented them to the 'Washerwoman', saying: *'If you can defeat "The Rabbit" and look good defeating him, I may give you an opportunity to be in a ten million dollar gate with me.'*

* * *

In December 1967 he was to fight the powerfully-built Argentinian Oscar Bonavena (nicknamed 'The Argentine Bull'), who called Ali a chicken. Ali's reply:

I promise to be the torero to Bonavena's bull and wear red trunks in the fight.

* * *

Asked to predict on the fight:

I tell you the Beast is mine
And tonight he falls in nine.
Before round nine is out,
The Ref will jump and shout:
'That's all, folks, this bull is out!'

★ ★ ★

His prediction of his October 1970 fight with Irish-American Jerry Quarry, said to be the best white boxer in the world:

The last of the Great White Hopes.

★ ★ ★

On Britain's great hope Joe Bugner:

Just watch out for Joe Bugner. He's gonna be one of the greatest – after *I'm through. He will hit and hurt any other heavyweight. He'll never meet another dancing master like me.*

★ ★ ★

Predicting on his February 1973 fight with Bugner:

'Man, who do you think you is - 'enery Cooper?'

'I'm the Greatest!'

Joe Bugner will be in heaven
When the round strikes seven.
And if he makes me sore
I'll cut it to four.

★ ★ ★

His warning to England regarding Joe Bugner's bid:

From all over the world they send their best
To battle Ali for the ultimate test.
Now merry olde England is sending her hero
Big Joe Bugner, whose chances are zero.
Now big Joe, he can swing, he can roll
But with Muhammad Ali in there, the ring is just too small.
Since when could a bug handle a bee,
A bee that's as pretty and as quick as me.
Bugs fly through the air with the greatest of ease,
But this is one bug who will be on his knees.
When I meet the bug I will have it made
*Because with me I will have a can of Raid.**
I always make predictions that come out right
And Bugner, don't bug me, and remember the day
This Valentine Day massacre will happen the same way.
So, Joe, you should say a good long prayer
Because this black Capone will be your slayer.

* An American insecticide

★ ★ ★

'Ah hears de gentle voices singing poor ol' Joe . . .'

He was prepared to accept an offer to go and fight exhibitions in South Africa, provided the audience would be 50–50 white and black.

I want them to see what a black man can do. Pity they won't let me go in with their white champion.

★ ★ ★

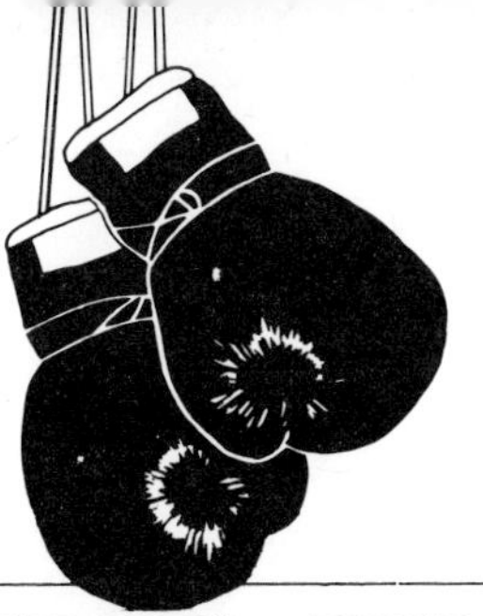

6. ON THE WORLD

ON INDIVIDUALS

Of his trainer Angelo Dundee:

I like him 'cause he's half-coloured. Got a lot of coloured nigger blood in him. Everybody likes him. He's got the connection and the complexion to get me the right protection which leads to good affection.

★ ★ ★

His reason for turning down a film part as Shaka, warrior chief of the Zulus:

He killed too many people.

★ ★ ★

When he visited a hospital and met six-year-old John Owens, who had apparently fallen off a wall and fractured his skull, Ali put his arms around him and said:

Now, John, you mustn't try playing Humpty Dumpty no more.

He visited a children's ward, and told the group of little amputees:

They can give you legs, and when you grow up you'll be doing the Ali shuffle.

* * *

When he visited Scotland in 1965, he was invited to visit the cottage of the poet Robert Burns. To his fans at an autograph session:

I am going to Burns' Cottage tomorrow to see if this fellow Bobby Burns was a better poet than I am.

* * *

His poem about Robert Burns after visiting his grave:

I'd heard of a man named Burns – supposed to be a poet;
But, if he was, how come I didn't know it?
They told me his work was very, very neat.
So I replied: 'But who did he ever beat?'

* * *

In 1970, in the company of the Press, he watched the then Vice-President of America, Spiro Agnew, playing tennis on television, accidentally hitting his partner with the ball on the head and his partner getting a helmet for protection. Ali declared:

Do you see what they do? They kill people in Asia, and shoot down college kids, black and white, and here is the guy who is part of it all and they're trying to make you think what a nice guy he is playing tennis.

* * *

ON WOMEN

Asked what role he thought women were created to play in life:

A man's woman is the field which produces his nation. If he don't protect his field, he don't protect his nation. Farmers study chemicals and poisons, they spray them on their cabbages, their corn, looking to kill any worm or insect which seeks to destroy his crops. And how much more important is a man's woman than his cabbage and his corn, when she is the field which produces his sons and daughters?

★ ★ ★

Asked if he did not think that black women would be happier with the progressive ideas of Women's Liberation than the teaching of his religion – which is to keep women in the home:

Black women don't pay no attention to Women's Liberation! I think it was something designed to keep black people down. Because usually what whites do, blacks follow. The white people see the black people in America uniting, and the quick way to divide a man is to take his woman from him – or give him trouble at home. Women's Liberation is a move to separate the woman from the man because if black women start joining in this type of independent talk, it will keep the man from getting powerful. But the Movement is dying because the black women pay no attention to it!

★ ★ ★

Commenting on Women's Liberation:

I see why the women of the Liberation feel as bad as they do. Look around . . . for instance at a great big beautiful home. They are called mansions – *not* she-shuns *or* peopleshuns, *and the women are very angry because of*

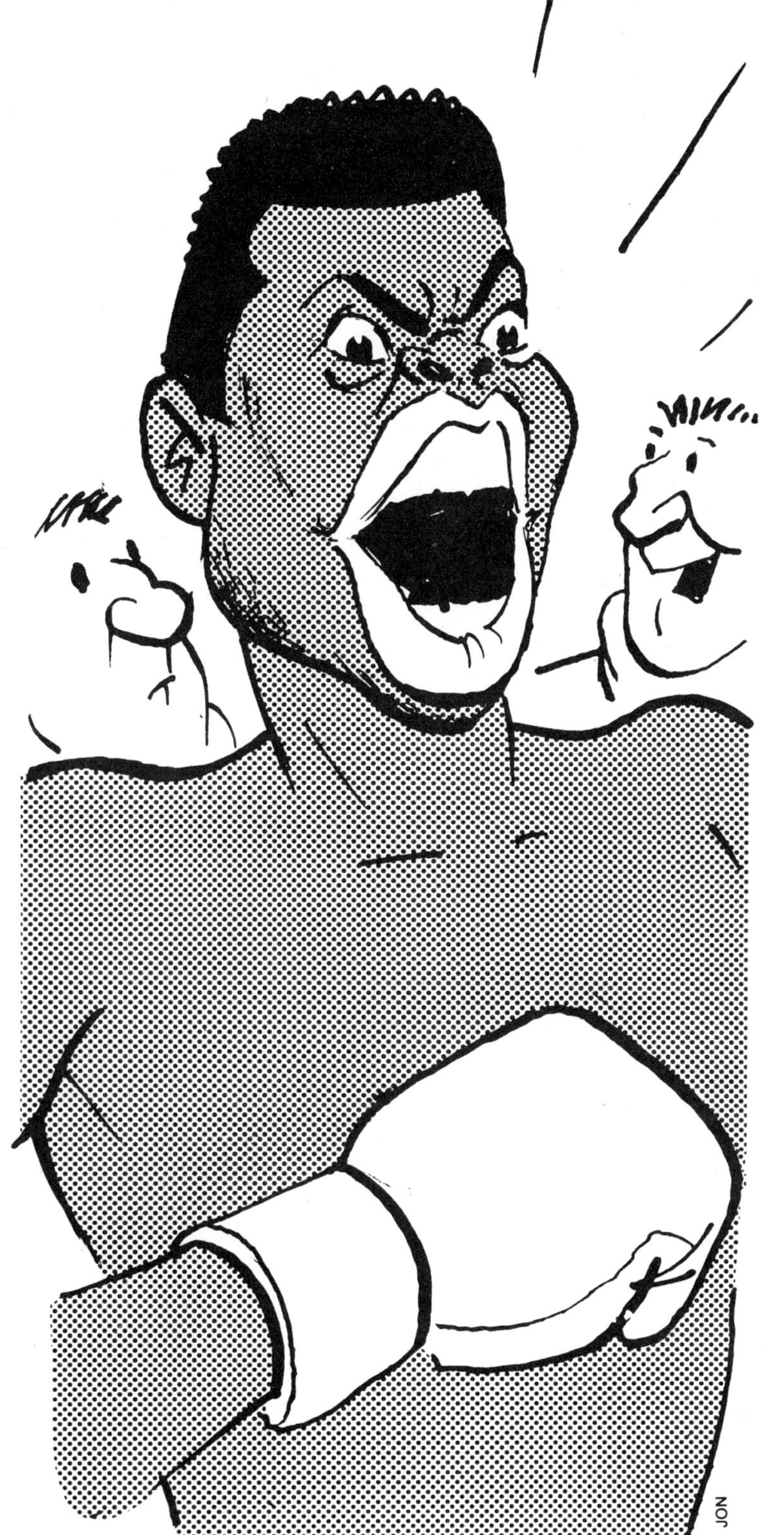

'He's just reassuring himself that his jaw isn't busted this time.'

that. If a man should get a ruptured bowel or intestine, they don't call it a his-ia, *they call it a* hernia. *And the women don't like that. If a person goes back in the woods and lives a sad dull life, you call him a* hermit. *Women think they should be called* his-its *or something. And another thing women don't like,* hurricanes *are destructive and they're named after women like Deidre and Carol and Sue. They don't call them* his-icanes *and they don't name them Bob or George or Bill. And women have certain kinds of illnesses but they don't call it* her-sterectomy, *they call it* hysterectomy. *If women do something great in* history *they don't call it* her-story. *Those are the kind of things that upset women. I think they should take down them Men and Women signs in toilets and just let everyone go where they want to! Amen . . . I mean,* Awomen *. . . I don't know, I'm confused!*

★ ★ ★

ON FOOD

His reasons for hating pork:

Do you think, my brother, in God's great plan
When he was prescribing the best food for man

That he made a mistake by leaving the swine out
For he was no good from the tail to the snout?

The carcass of a old dead horse or a cow
Don't get too rotten for the dirty ol' sow.

We couldn't eat a buzzard, we would think it was a crime
But how much more filthy is he than the swine?

We cook him with cabbage, boil him in greens,
With his mangey ol' hide we season our beans.

On filth they feast, while in stink holes they lay
And still for their carcass our money we pay.

We may like them lean or we may like them best fat
Just as well eat a dog or a cat!

Our most sensitive natures would almost run wild
If we ate the carcass of a man or a child.

The dirtiest of beasts we will not do without
We eat the whole hog from the tail to the snout.

Yes, we worship the Lord, and we pay and we shout
But that ol' hog flavour we can't do without.

We'd be better off if we obeyed God's command and
Ate vegetables and grain and fruit of the land.

You may think fresh pork is a very rare treat
But our bodies are made of just what we eat.

And the food that the hog has eaten, which is the filth of the land
Goes into our body as second hand.

Now I've told you my story, recited my piece
And if you can eat pork with your conscience at ease
If sin, filth and disease you care little about
Then keep on eating the brute from the tail to the snout!

ON RACE RELATIONS

After winning the 1960 Gold Medal at the Rome Olympics, Ali was approached by a Russian reporter who asked: 'How does it feel to win something for a country where you can't eat at the same table with a white man?' Ali furiously replied: 'Tell your readers we got qualified people working on that and I'm not worried about the outcome. The USA is still the best country in the world.' Ali said later:

That man went away with nothing to write in his Russian papers. That Russian probably thought, 'That's a bad nigger'.

★ ★ ★

In a television interview with David Frost:

ALI: *All whites are devils.*

FROST: How about people like Abraham Lincoln and President Kennedy who have done some good for black people? Were they devils? Would you call President Kennedy a devil?

ALI: *Well, was President Kennedy a white man?*

★ ★ ★

Asked why he opposed racial integration:

Everything with common sense wants to be with his own. Bluebirds with bluebirds, redbirds with redbirds, pigeons with pigeons, eagles with eagles, tigers with tigers, monkeys with monkeys. As small as an ant's brain is, red ants want to be with red ants, black ants with black ants.

★ ★ ★

On the colour of Jesus Christ:

I remember right in our house back in Louisville all the pictures on the walls were white people. Nothing about us black people. A picture of a white Jesus Christ. Now what painter ever saw Jesus? So who says Jesus is white?

★ ★ ★

One of his reasons for refusing to go and fight in Vietnam:

I don't have no quarrel with them Vietcongs. The Vietcongs don't call me nigger.

★ ★ ★

His defence when the press were criticising his refusal to go and fight in Vietnam:

You want me to do what the white man says and go fight a war against some other people I don't know nothing about, get some freedom for some other people when my own people can't get theirs here?

On the question of colour:

Poor black man, he been over a long, hard road. It probably started back when his momma dragged him to the Baptist Church or the Catholic Church, and he first saw Jesus. He saw a white man, with a hair like no Negro ever had. Later on, he look at the Last Supper. He see everybody at the table look like Jesus' kin. No Chinese at the Last Supper, no Mexicans, all white people. Then he look at the angels in Heaven and they're all white, and he don't see no pictures of black people dying and going up to heaven to join those blond angels. And he look at the story-books and everybody good is white. And Miss America is white and Miss World is white and Miss Universe is white and the President, he lives in the White House. And the Angel cake is white and the devil cake is black. Only thing he know is that Africa is black, the jungles of Africa are black. And who do he find out is the King of Africa? Ahhhh-ooooo-aaah, it's Tarzan! A white man swinging through Africa with a draper.

★ ★ ★

On the pride of being black:

I got to make the grown-up black child who's never seen nothing good about black feel like he's something. 'Say brother,' I ask, 'do you know black is original? Do you know all other colours come out of black? From the black man comes the brown man and the yellow and the white. Did you know you're the father of all men? Did you know black was here before God? Doesn't the Book say that before God created the heavens and the earth everything was covered in darkness? And what colour is darkness? Did you know the strong dirt, the rich dirt, is black soil? Did you know the blacker the berry, the sweeter the juice? The strong coffee is the black coffee and it don't get weak till you integrate it with cream.

ON ENGLAND

When he was shown Buckingham Palace:

Gee! That's a mighty swell pad.

* * *

When Oxford University asked him to become their Professor of Poetry after world-wide speculation that his defeat by Ken Norton had ended his career, Ali replied:

Pay heed, my children, and you will see
Why this is not the time for your university.
It's not the pay, although that's small
But I have to show the world I can still walk tall.

* * *

7. ON GEORGE FOREMAN

In October 1974 Muhammad Ali, at the age of 32, regained the world Heavyweight Championship by beating George Foreman by a knock-out in the eighth round. Here is his prediction of the then-impending fight:

Oh, Muhammad comes out to meet George Foreman, but George starts to retreat.
If Foreman goes back farther, he will wind up in a ringside seat.

Ali swings with a left, Ali swings with a right.
Look at the Champ take the fight!

George keeps backing, but there's not enough room. It's a matter of time.
Now he lowers the boom. Now he lands with a right.

What a beautiful swing!
And the punch lifts George clean out of the ring.

Foreman is still rising, but the Ref wears a frown
For he can't start counting till George comes down.

Now George disappears from view. The crowd is getting frantic.
But our radar stations have picked him up. He's somewhere over the Atlantic.

Who would have thought when they came to the fight
That they would witness the launching of a black satellite?

★ ★ ★

After the fight:

Man, I was perfect.

★ ★ ★

The contest took place in Zaire in front of a delirious African crowd who chanted: 'Ali boma ye – Ali kill him'. The new champion asked:

In all your life did you see a man jab so pretty and quick as old Muhammad Ali did?

★ ★ ★

I was going straight out but using my brains. Did you see that timing of mine? Man, it was perfect.

★ ★ ★

Once the howitzer blows, which had been so powerful for 40 previous opponents, failed to flatten, Foreman was lost. He wasn't helped by Ali's unflattering commentary on his efforts:

George, where's your big punch?
George, you're hitting like a cissy.

★ ★ ★

Ali insisted afterwards that the snarl he directed at Foreman was only a mild rebuke:

You're fighting dirty, George. You shouldn't do it.

★ ★ ★

On his tactics during the fight:

The trick was to make him think he was the baddest man in the world and everybody had to run from him. Truth is I could have killed myself dancin' against him. He's too big for me to keep moving round him. I was a bit winded after doin' it in the first round, so I said to myself 'Let me get to the ropes while I'm fresh, while I can handle him there without gettin' hurt. Let him burn himself out. Let him blast his ass off and pray he keeps throwin'. Let it be a matter of who can hit who first, and that's me.' This was a real scientific fight, a real thinkin' fight. For me it was. Everythin' I did had a purpose.
There he was wingin' away and all the time I was talkin' to him sayin', 'Hit harder, George. That was the best you got? They told me you had body punches but that don't hurt even a little bit. Harder, sucker, swing harder. You the champion and you gettin' nowhere. Now I'm gonna jab you.' Then pop! I'd stick him with a jab. 'I'm gonna jab you again sucker,' I'd say and there it'd go. Pop! 'Nothin' you can do about it, sucker.' He didn't like gettin' hit with those punches. You see his head go on his shoulders, you see it turn every time I connected? And when did I miss?

I'd jab, then give him a right cross, then finish with a jab. Nobody expects you to finish a combination with a jab. Those punches took the heart away from George. Joe Frazier mighta taken them but they sickened George. When he did all that talkin' about concentratin' on his defence because he was scary about takin' punishment people thought he was just a big man kiddin' along. But he really don't like punishment and I proved it.
By the fifth round, you remember, when I leaned back on the ropes and gave him all the free shots he wanted and he couldn't do nothin' to bother me, by then I knew George had shot his load. I knew he was through.

★ ★ ★

On the possibility of a rematch:

I'm gonna get a lot of credit for something I don't deserve. He's not a great fighter, no sir. Mind you, you must never underestimate me.
If we have a rematch, I might get him in three rounds. Now I know he can go. I never had to dance. That was my ace. And right now, the world is happy because I made it happy.
You saw the power of Allah, not me. I'm not known for being a hitter but I said you would see the greatest surprise in the history of boxing, a miracle.
A rematch? Yeah, Ah'll give him one but he won't have a chance. He knows that now. He's afraid of me now. Did you see how he was afraid when he got into the ring?

★ ★ ★

Within minutes of the end of the fight, Ali spoke half to himself in his dressing room:

I'll tell you my secret. It is this. I make any man who comes against me lose his confidence.
Foreman couldn't look me in the eyes at first and when he did he looked deep. *Then he knew – he knew I was someone different.*

★ ★ ★

He spoke about Foreman's famous punches:

Were you scared when I let him punch away at me like that? It weren't nothin'. He weren't hittin' no spots, no place vital where he could hurt me. I was leanin' back over the ropes with my head out of the way and my arms were savin' me from real damage on the body. If he'd hurt me, I'd have moved. I knew what I was doin'. You know I wouldn't go in there to let no street fighter mess me around.

★ ★ ★

After the fight the champion watched a television cassette of a fight preview with rapt, boyish attention. When he wasn't arguing with the comments of others he was calling for proper respect to be shown to his own contributions:

Shhhhh ... Listen to me here ... Watch this ... I was right, wasn't I? ... I said I'd stop him after seven and he went eight ... I even cancelled the rain. It stayed dry for the fight, then an hour after it there was a storm that nearly flooded the place.

He bent over the set with hostile concentration when Foreman's manager, Dick Sadler, came up on the screen. Sadler said his man was a thunderous, murderous puncher. Ali said flatly:

No he ain't.

★ ★ ★

Sadler was then shown holding a heavy bag while the former champion went close to punching a hole in it. Ali said:

Trouble was, no-one was holding me!

★ ★ ★

And about his own punch:

I'm the man who can't punch. Ask George Foreman.

★ ★ ★

This is how he summed up the contest:

I have been boxing 20 years and I'm a pretty good fighter. I can walk into the firin' line with a man like Foreman and I got no fear. Nothin' can happen that I don't understand. I been to school.
I was a pro nine years before he was. When he got knocked down it was

new to him and he was lost. I've been down. I've been humiliated. Had my title taken away. Had my jaw broke. Had so much trouble with my hands for seven years now the doctors been tellin' me to quit. This time they were strong. I was able to hit the heavy bag and I fought without Novocaine injections for the first time in years. But I been through all these things. I know the hard side.

It was an amateur against a professional, a kid against a man. I tell you somethin', if he had got up I could have humiliated that boy. George has been actin' up with fancy clothes and all that stuff with his dog, and misusin' people, runnin' the Press around, talkin' funny when he does talk. He used to be a nice fella but he's changin'. You know how big it makes me to get the title back ten years after I won it from that other big bad bully Liston, to be just the second man to regain the heavyweight championship and the first to win it twice without ever losin' it in the ring. Yet you can walk in on me here and talk to me, no sweat. Tomorrow I'll be back in the ghetto pickin' up black babies and drinkin' soda at a corner store. I talk plenty but I don't act up like George.

★ ★ ★

After the fight he mused:

Muhammad Ali stops George Foreman. Man, that is a hell of a upset. It will be weeks before I realise the impact of this. I don't feel like I'm champion again yet. I can't wait to see all them magazines. They got *to say I'm the greatest now, the greatest of all times. I fooled them all.*

★ ★ ★

Ali had promised that, win or lose, he would retire after the Foreman fight. He was going to give up boxing to become a minister in the

Black Muslim faith under the leadership of Elijah Muhammad. Now, having won back the championship, he said:

Retirement? I'll sit on it for a while.

★ ★ ★

I intend to haunt the world of boxing for the next six months with the fear that I will retire.

★ ★ ★

If any man has ten million dollars, then I will think about fighting again.
Meanwhile I will halt the world of boxing for six months.
I shall not retire before then so my name will be shown as heavyweight champion in next year's record books.

★ ★ ★

Governments are looking for me now, not promoters.

★ ★ ★

Newspapers everywhere carried the message: 'Ali proved this morning that he is the greatest champion in the history of boxing. No man could be more.' Ali agrees:

I told you I was the greatest of all time. Never again say I'm going to be defeated. Never again make me an underdog until I'm 50 years of age. All of you suckers bow. Now you have to recognise me as the scholar of boxing.

ACKNOWLEDGEMENTS

Every effort has been made to trace the ownership of all copyright material in this book, and the Publishers express their sincere apologies if they have innocently erred.

The Publishers are grateful to the authors, publishers, and editors who have allowed them to quote from their works, and for the interest they have shown in the research.

Acknowledgements are due to the following:

ROY ULLYETT, London Express Newspapers Limited and their Syndication Department for their help with the cartoon content of this book.

JON and the Editor of the London *Daily Mail* for their assistance with cartoons.

ROY HEELAS for his photo captions.

JOSE TORRES, *Sting Like A Bee* – Abelard-Schuman; copyright Jose Torres & Bert Randolph Sugar.

BUDD SCHULBERG, *Loser & Still Champion – Muhammad Ali* – New English Library; Doubleday & Company Inc, USA; copyright Budd Schulberg.

TOM WOLFE, *The Kandy-Kolored Tangerine-Flake Streamline Baby* – Jonathan Cape; copyright Tom Wolfe.

Walter Bartleman and the Editor of the London *Evening Standard.*

The Editor of the *Scottish Daily Express.*

Mike Jay and the Editor of *The Daily World,* New York.

Alan Hoby and the Editor of the London *Sunday Express.*

Frank McGhee and the Editor of the London *Daily Mirror.*

Norman Gilier and the Editor of the London *Daily Express.*